First
Facts®

The
Most Adorable
ANIMALS
IN THE WORLD

by Tammy Gagne

raintree 🍃

a Capstone company — publishers for children

Raintree is an imprint of Capstone Global Library Limited, a company incorporated in England and Wales having its registered office at 7 Pilgrim Street, London, EC4V 6LB – Registered company number: 6695582

www.raintree.co.uk
myorders@raintree.co.uk

Editorial Credits
Kathryn Clay, editor; Bobbie Nuytten, designer; Jo Miller, media researcher; Kathy McColley, production specialist

ISBN 978 1 4062 9310 4
18 17 16 15 14
10 9 8 7 6 5 4 3 2 1

British Library Cataloguing in Publication Data
A full catalogue record for this book is available from the British Library.

Photo Credits
iStockphotos: charmedesign, 5, 22, Craig Dingle, 19, 22; Shutterstock: Cat Downie, cover (bottom right), Eric Gevaert, 21, 22, hjschneider, 15, 22, iravgustin, 14, Joe Ravi, cover (middle), 7, 22, Martchan, cover (top), 1, meunierd, 13, 22, nattanan726, 11, 22, Robyn Mackenzie, 18, sevenke, 6, Sourav and Joyeeta, 10, Tory Kallman, 17, 22, Vladimir Melnik, cover (bottom left), 9, 22, wormig, 22 (map)

Printed in China.
0914/CA21401516

Table of Contents

Quokka

Large or small. Fluffy or feathered. Animals have physical **traits** that set them apart from one another. Some traits make animals look scary or unfriendly. Other traits are simply adorable. The quokka always appears to be smiling. Unlike many wild animals, this Australian **marsupial** is known for being extremely friendly.

trait feature or quality about something that makes it different from others

marsupial group of mammals in which the females feed and carry their young in pouches

Fact: Most quokkas are found on Rottnest Island, off the south-west coast of Australia.

Red Panda

Many people are surprised by the red panda's appearance. Found in China, red pandas look more like raccoons than pandas. Their red and white colouring provides **camouflage** in the bamboo forests where they live.

camouflage pattern or colour on an animal that helps it to blend in with the things around it

Fact: Red pandas have soft fur all over their bodies. Even the soles of their feet are covered with fur.

7

Harp Seal

Adorable animals live on land and in the sea. The harp seal lives in the North Atlantic and Arctic Oceans. Baby harp seals have white fur. The thick fur coat and layer of **blubber** keep the animals warm in icy waters. The fluffy white fur is also valuable. Many harp seals are hunted each year for their prized **pelts**.

blubber thick layer of fat under the skin of some animals; blubber keeps animals warm

pelt animal's skin with the hair or fur still on it

Fact: Mother harp seals can find their babies among hundreds of others just by scent.

Fennec Fox

The fennec fox of northern Africa has huge, pointed ears. The long ears remove heat from the animal's body during hot days in the desert. A long, thick coat keeps the fox warm at night.

Fact: Fennec foxes are the smallest members of the Canidae family. This group includes wolves, coyotes and dogs.

Chinchilla

Wild chinchillas live in the Andes Mountains of South America. They have the softest fur of all **mammals**. Their fur is sometimes used to make clothing. Because of over-hunting, chinchillas are now considered to be **endangered**.

mammal warm–blooded animal that breathes air; mammals have hair or fur; female mammals feed milk to their young

endangered at risk of dying out

Fact: To clean their fur, chinchillas roll around in dust. The dust soaks up oil and dirt.

Alpaca

Like chinchillas, wild alpacas live in the mountains of South America. Some people raise these friendly, gentle animals on farms. Their fleece is used to make yarn for clothing. Many farms even allow families to come and see the animals.

Fact: Alpaca fleece is softer than cashmere and warmer than wool.

Bottlenose Dolphin

Bottlenose dolphins are not only cute. They are also among the smartest creatures in the world. These members of the whale family are quite social. They live in groups of 2 to 15, and communicate with one other through sound. Each dolphin has a unique whistle. Scientists have found that dolphins use these sounds to identify one another.

Koala

The koala is often called a koala "bear" by mistake. But this cuddly animal is actually a marsupial, like the quokka. Koalas live in **eucalyptus** trees in Australia. Because they eat the trees' leaves, most koalas rarely even come down to the ground. They get most of their water from the eucalyptus leaves.

eucalyptus strong-smelling evergreen tree that grows in dry climates

Fact: A koala can eat as much as 1 kilogram (2.5 pounds) of eucalyptus leaves every day.

Emperor Tamarin

The emperor tamarin appears to have a long, white moustache. This small type of monkey lives in the forests of South America. Emperor tamarins are social animals that live together in troops. Each troop has two to eight members and is led by the oldest female.

Fact: The emperor tamarin got its name from a Swiss scientist. The scientist joked that the animal looked like the former German Emperor Wilhelm II. The Emperor also had a long moustache.

Habitat Map

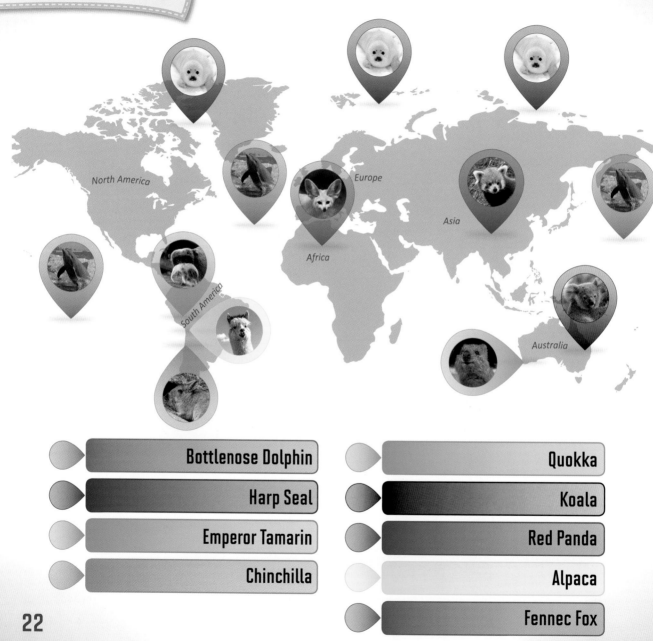

- Bottlenose Dolphin
- Harp Seal
- Emperor Tamarin
- Chinchilla
- Quokka
- Koala
- Red Panda
- Alpaca
- Fennec Fox

North America

South America

Europe

Africa

Asia

Australia

Glossary

blubber thick layer of fat under the skin of some animals; blubber keeps animals warm

camouflage pattern or colour on an animal that helps it blend in with the things around it

endangered at risk of dying out

eucalyptus strong-smelling evergreen tree that grows in dry climates

mammal warm–blooded animal that breathes air; mammals have hair or fur; female mammals feed milk to their young

marsupial group of mammals in which the females feed and carry their young in pouches

pelt animal's skin with the hair or fur still on it

trait feature or quality about something that makes it different from others

Comprehension Questions

1. How does a red fox blend in with its environment?

2. Reread page 12 about how chinchillas are considered endangered. What can people do to protect chinchillas?

Books

125 Cute Animals, National Geographic Kids (National Geographic Society, 2015)

Dolphins (Living in the Wild: Sea Mammals), Anna Claybourne (Raintree Publishers, 2014)

Fennec Fox (A Day in the Life: Desert Animals), Anita Ganeri (Raintree Publishers, 2011)

Websites

www.ngkids.co.uk
Learn about all types of animals, including information about their physical features, habitats and behaviours.

www.bristolzoo.org.uk/learning-resources
Find out more about animals, zoos and endangered species. Take a look at the Animal and Habitat fact sheets to learn more about seals, red pandas and other adorable animals.

Index